D1189881

WILLIAM BLAKE

Selected Poems

BLOOMSBURY
★ POETRY ★
CLASSICS

St. Martin's Press
New York

Selection by Ian Hamilton
Jacket design by Jeff Fisher

ISBN 0-312-11937-2

First published in Great Britain by Bloomsbury Publishing Ltd.

First U.S. Edition: March 1995
10 9 8 7 6 5 4 3 2 1

CONTENTS

To Spring 9

To the Evening Star 10

Song ('How sweet I roamed') 11

Song ('My silks and fine array') 12

Song ('Love and harmony combine') 13

Song ('Memory, hither come') 14

Mad Song 15

Song ('Fresh from the dewy hill') 16

Song ('When early morn') 17

To the Muses 18

Thel's Motto 19

Introduction (to *Songs of Innocence*) 20

The Shepherd 21

The Ecchoing Green 22

The Lamb 24

The Little Black Boy 25

The Chimney Sweeper 27

The Little Boy Lost 29

The Little Boy Found 30

A Cradle Song 31

Holy Thursday 33

Night 34

Nurse's Song 36

Infant Joy 37

A Dream 38

On Anothers Sorrow 39

Introduction (to *Songs of Experience*) 41

Earth's Answer	42
The Clod and the Pebble	44
Holy Thursday	45
The Little Girl Lost	46
The Little Girl Found	49
The Chimney Sweeper	52
Nurses Song	53
The Sick Rose	54
The Fly	55
The Tyger	56
My Pretty Rose Tree	58
Ah! Sun-Flower	59
The Lilly	60
London	61
The Human Abstract	62
Infant Sorrow	63
A Little Boy Lost	64
A Little Girl Lost	66
To Tirzah	68
The Voice of the Ancient Bard	69
From the Notebooks	70
Eternity	71
Auguries of Innocence	72
The Mental Traveller	77
From *Vala – or the Four Zoas*	
1. Enion and Tharmas	82
2. Enion's Lament	83
3. Terrific Urizen	85
4. Vala's Lament	88

5. Enion's Second Lament	89
6. Enion, from the Caverns of the Grave	92
7. Vala's Song	96
The Smile	98
The Golden Net	99
The Land of Dreams	100
Mary	101
The Crystal Cabinet	104
William Bond	106
From *Visions of the Daughters of Albion*	109
From *America*	113
Jerusalem (from *Milton*)	114
From *Milton* 2 ('Thou hearest the Nightingale . . .')	115
From *Milton* 3 ('When I first married you . . .')	118
From *Jerusalem* 2 ('And many conversed . . .')	119
From *Jerusalem* 2 To the Jews	121
Epigraph to To The Christians	126
Epilogue	127

TO SPRING

O thou, with dewy locks, who lookest down
Thro' the clear windows of the morning; turn
Thine angel eyes upon our western isle,
Which in full choir hails thy approach, O Spring!

The hills tell each other, and the list'ning
Vallies hear; all our longing eyes are turned
Up to thy bright pavillions: issue forth,
And let thy holy feet visit our clime.

Come o'er the eastern hills, and let our winds
Kiss thy perfumed garments; let us taste
Thy morn and evening breath; scatter thy pearls
Upon our love-sick land that mourns for thee.

O deck her forth with thy fair fingers; pour
Thy soft kisses on her bosom; and put
Thy golden crown upon her languish'd head,
Whose modest tresses were bound up for thee!

TO THE EVENING STAR

Thou fair-hair'd angel of the evening,
Now, while the sun rests on the mountains, light
Thy bright torch of love; thy radiant crown
Put on, and smile upon our evening bed!
Smile on our loves; and, while thou drawest the
Blue curtains of the sky, scatter thy silver dew
On every flower that shuts its sweet eyes
In timely sleep. Let thy west wind sleep on
The lake; speak silence with thy glimmering eyes,
And wash the dusk with silver. Soon, full soon,
Dost thou withdraw; then the wolf rages wide,
And the lion glares thro' the dun forest:
The fleeces of our flocks are cover'd with
Thy sacred dew: protect them with thine influence.

SONG

How sweet I roam'd from field to field,
  And tasted all the summer's pride,
'Till I the prince of love beheld,
  Who in the sunny beams did glide!

He shew'd me lilies for my hair,
  And blushing roses for my brow;
He led me through his gardens fair,
  Where all his golden pleasures grow.

With sweet May dews my wings were wet,
  And Phoebus fir'd my vocal rage;
He caught me in his silken net,
  And shut me in his golden cage.

He loves to sit and hear me sing,
  Then, laughing, sports and plays with me;
Then stretches out my golden wing,
  And mocks my loss of liberty.

SONG

My silks and fine array,
  My smiles and languish'd air,
By love are driv'n away;
  And mournful lean Despair
Brings me yew to deck my grave:
Such end true lovers have.

His face is fair as heav'n,
  When springing buds unfold;
O why to him was't giv'n,
  Whose heart is wintry cold?
His breast is love's all worship'd tomb,
Where all love's pilgrims come.

Bring me an axe and spade,
  Bring me a winding sheet;
When I my grave have made,
  Let winds and tempests beat:
Then down I'll lie, as cold as clay.
True love doth pass away!

SONG

Love and harmony combine,
And around our souls intwine,
While thy branches mix with mine,
And our roots together join.

Joys upon our branches sit,
Chirping loud, and singing sweet;
Like gentle streams beneath our feet
Innocence and virtue meet.

Thou the golden fruit dost bear,
I am clad in flowers fair;
Thy sweet boughs perfume the air,
And the turtle buildeth there.

There she sits and feeds her young,
Sweet I hear her mournful song;
And thy lovely leaves among,
There is love: I hear his tongue.

There his charming nest doth lay,
There he sleeps the night away;
There he sports along the day,
And doth among our branches play.

SONG

Memory, hither come,
   And tune your merry notes;
And, while upon the wind,
   Your music floats,
I'll pore upon the stream,
Where sighing lovers dream,
And fish for fancies as they pass
Within the watery glass.

I'll drink of the clear stream,
   And hear the linnet's song;
And there I'll lie and dream
   The day along:
And, when night comes, I'll go
   To places fit for woe;
Walking along the darken'd valley,
   With silent Melancholy.

MAD SONG

The wild winds weep,
   And the night is a-cold;
Come hither, Sleep,
   And my griefs infold:
But lo! the morning peeps
   Over the eastern steeps,
And the rustling birds of dawn
The earth do scorn.

Lo! to the vault
   Of paved heaven,
With sorrow fraught
   My notes are driven:
They strike the ear of night,
   Make weep the eyes of day;
They make mad the roaring winds,
   And with tempests play.

Like a fiend in a cloud
   With howling woe,
After night I do croud,
   And with night will go;
I turn my back to the east,
From whence comforts have increas'd;
For light doth seize my brain
With frantic pain.

SONG

Fresh from the dewy hill, the merry year
Smiles on my head, and mounts his flaming car;
Round my young brows the laurel wreathes a shade,
And rising glories beam around my head.

My feet are wing'd, while o'er the dewy lawn,
I meet my maiden, risen like the morn:
Oh bless those holy feet, like angels' feet;
Oh bless those limbs, beaming with heav'nly light!

Like as an angel glitt'ring in the sky,
In times of innocence, and holy joy;
The joyful shepherd stops his grateful song,
To hear the music of an angel's tongue.

So when she speaks, the voice of Heaven I hear
So when we walk, nothing impure comes near;
Each field seems Eden, and each calm retreat;
Each village seems the haunt of holy feet.

But that sweet village where my black-ey'd maid,
Closes her eyes in sleep beneath night's shade:
Whene'er I enter, more than mortal fire
Burns in my soul, and does my song inspire.

SONG

When early morn walks forth in sober grey;
Then to my black ey'd maid I haste away,
When evening sits beneath her dusky bow'r,
And gently sighs away the silent hour;
The village bell alarms, away I go;
And the vale darkens at my pensive woe.

To that sweet village, where my black ey'd maid
Doth drop a tear beneath the silent shade,
I turn my eyes; and, pensive as I go,
Curse my black stars, and bless my pleasing woe.

Oft when the summer sleeps among the trees,
Whisp'ring faint murmurs to the scanty breeze,
I walk the village round; if at her side
A youth doth walk in stolen joy and pride,
I curse my stars in bitter grief and woe,
That made my love so high, and me so low.

O should she e'er prove false, his limbs I'd tear,
And throw all pity on the burning air;
I'd curse bright fortune for my mixed lot,
And then I'd die in peace, and be forgot.

TO THE MUSES

Whether on Ida's shady brow,
   Or in the chambers of the East,
The chambers of the sun, that now
   From antient melody have ceas'd;

Whether in Heav'n ye wander fair,
   Or the green corners of the earth,
Or the blue regions of the air,
   Where the melodious winds have birth;

Whether on chrystal rocks ye rove,
   Beneath the bosom of the sea
Wand'ring in many a coral grove,
   Fair Nine, forsaking Poetry!

How have you left the antient love
   That bards of old enjoy'd in you!
The languid strings do scarcely move!
   The sound is forc'd, the notes are few!

THEL'S MOTTO

Does the Eagle know what is in the pit?
Or wilt thou go ask the Mole:
Can Wisdom be put in a silver rod?
Or Love in a golden bowl?

SONGS OF INNOCENCE

INTRODUCTION

Piping down the valleys wild
Piping songs of pleasant glee
On a cloud I saw a child.
And he laughing said to me:

Pipe a song about a Lamb;
So I piped with merry chear,
Piper pipe that song again –
So I piped, he wept to hear.

Drop thy pipe thy happy pipe
Sing thy songs of happy chear,
So I sung the same again
While he wept with joy to hear

Piper sit thee down and write
In a book that all may read –
So he vanish'd from my sight.
And I pluck'd a hollow reed.

And I made a rural pen,
And I stain'd the water clear,
And I wrote my happy songs
Every child may joy to hear

THE SHEPHERD

How sweet is the Shepherds sweet lot,
From the morn to the evening he strays:
He shall follow his sheep all the day
And his tongue shall be filled with praise.

For he hears the lambs innocent call.
And he hears the ewes tender reply.
He is watchful while they are in peace.
For they know when their Shepherd is nigh.

THE ECCHOING GREEN

The Sun does arise,
And make happy the skies.
The merry bells ring
To welcome the Spring.
The sky-lark and thrush,
The birds of the bush,
Sing louder around.
To the bells chearful sound.
While our sports shall be seen
On the Ecchoing Green.

Old John with white hair
Does laugh away care,
Sitting under the oak,
Among the old folk,
They laugh at our play,
And soon they all say:
Such such were the joys.
When we all girls & boys,
In our youth-time were seen,
On the Ecchoing Green.

Till the little ones weary
No more can be merry
The sun does descend.
And our sports have an end:
Round the laps of their mothers,
Many sisters and brothers,
Like birds in their nest,
Are ready for rest;
And sport no more seen,
On the darkening Green.

THE LAMB

Little Lamb who made thee
  Dost thou know who made thee
Gave thee life & bid thee feed.
By the stream & o'er the mead;
Gave thee clothing of delight,
Softest clothing wooly bright;
Gave thee such a tender voice,
Making all the vales rejoice:
  Little Lamb who made thee
  Dost thou know who made thee

Little Lamb I'll tell thee,
  Little Lamb I'll tell thee:
He is called by thy name,
For he calls himself a Lamb:
He is meek & he is mild,
He became a little child:
I a child & thou a lamb,
We are called by his name.
  Little Lamb God bless thee.
  Little Lamb God bless thee.

THE LITTLE BLACK BOY

My mother bore me in the southern wild,
And I am black, but O! my soul is white;
White as an angel is the English child:
But I am black as if bereav'd of light.

My mother taught me underneath a tree
And sitting down before the heat of day,
She took me on her lap and kissed me,
And pointing to the east began to say:

Look on the rising sun: there God does live
And gives his light, and gives his heat away.
And flowers and trees and beasts and men recieve
Comfort in morning joy in the noon day.

And we are put on earth a little space,
That we may learn to bear the beams of love,
And these black bodies and this sun-burnt face
Is but a cloud, and like a shady grove.

For when our souls have learn'd the heat to bear
The cloud will vanish we shall hear his voice.
Saying: come out from the grove my love & care,
And round my golden tent like lambs rejoice.

Thus did my mother say and kissed me,
And thus I say to little English boy:
When I from black and he from white cloud free,
And round the tent of God like lambs we joy:

Ill shade him from the heat till he can bear
To lean in joy upon our fathers knee.
And then I'll stand and stroke his silver hair,
And be like him and he will then love me.

THE CHIMNEY SWEEPER

When my mother died I was very young,
And my father sold me while yet my tongue,
Could scarcely cry weep weep weep weep.
So your chimneys I sweep & in soot I sleep.

Theres little Tom Dacre, who cried when his head
That curl'd like a lambs back, was shav'd, so I said:
Hush Tom never mind it, for when your head's bare,
You know that the soot cannot spoil your white
    hair.

And so he was quiet, & that very night,
As Tom was a sleeping he had such a sight,
That thousands of sweepers Dick, Joe Ned & Jack
Were all of them lock'd up in coffins of black

And by came an Angel who had a bright key,
And he open'd the coffins & set them all free.
Then down a green plain leaping laughing they run
And wash in a river and shine in the Sun.

Then naked & white, all their bags left behind,
They rise upon clouds, and sport in the wind.
And the Angel told Tom if he'd be a good boy,
He'd have God for his father & never want joy.

And so Tom awoke and we rose in the dark
And got with our bags & our brushes to work.
Tho' the morning was cold, Tom was happy & warm,
So if all do their duty, they need not fear harm.

THE LITTLE BOY LOST

Father, father, where are you going
O do not walk so fast.
Speak father, speak to your little boy
Or else I shall be lost,

The night was dark no father was there
The child was wet with dew.
The mire was deep, & the child did weep
And away the vapour flew.

THE LITTLE BOY FOUND

The little boy lost in the lonely fen,
Led by the wand'ring light,
Began to cry, but God ever nigh,
Appeard like his father in white.

He kissed the child & by the hand led
And to his mother brought,
Who in sorrow pale, thro' the lonely dale
Her little boy weeping sought.

A CRADLE SONG

Sweet dreams form a shade,
O'er my lovely infants head.
Sweet dreams of pleasant streams.
By happy silent moony beams.

Sweet sleep with soft down,
Weave thy brows an infant crown.
Sweet sleep Angel mild,
Hover o'er my happy child.

Sweet smiles in the night,
Hover over my delight.
Sweet smiles Mothers smiles
All the livelong night beguiles.

Sweet moans, dovelike sighs,
Chase not slumber from thy eyes.
Sweet moans, sweeter smiles.
All the dovelike moans beguiles.

Sleep sleep happy child.
All creation slept and smil'd.
Sleep sleep. happy sleep.
While o'er thee thy mother weep

Sweet babe in thy face,
Holy image I can trace.
Sweet babe once like thee,
Thy maker lay and wept for me

Wept for me for thee for all.
When he was an infant small.
Thou his image ever see.
Heavenly face that smiles on thee.

Smiles on thee on me on all,
Who became an infant small.
Infant smiles are his own smiles.
Heaven & earth to peace beguiles.

HOLY THURSDAY

Twas on a Holy Thursday their innocent faces clean
The children walking two & two in red & blue &
   green
Grey headed beadles walkd before with wands as white
   as snow
Till into the high dome of Pauls they like Thames
   waters flow

O what a multitude they seemd these flowers of
   London town
Seated in companies they sit with radiance all their
   own
The hum of multitudes was there but multitudes of
   lambs
Thousands of little boys & girls raising their innocent
   hands

Now like a mighty wind they raise to heaven the voice
   of song
Or like harmonious thunderings the seats of heaven
   among
Beneath them sit the aged men wise guardians of the
   poor
Then cherish pity, lest you drive an angel from your
   door

NIGHT

The sun descending in the west
The evening star does shine.
The birds are silent in their nest,
And I must seek for mine,
The moon like a flower,
In heavens high bower;
With silent delight,
Sits and smiles on the night.

Farewell green fields and happy groves,
Where flocks have took delight;
Where lambs have nibbled, silent moves
The feet of angels bright;
Unseen they pour blessing,
And joy without ceasing,
On each bud and blossom,
And each sleeping bosom.

They look in every thoughtless nest,
Where birds are coverd warm;
They visit caves of every beast,
To keep them all from harm;
If they see any weeping,
That should have been sleeping
They pour sleep on their head
And sit down by their bed.

When wolves and tygers howl for prey
They pitying stand and weep;
Seeking to drive their thirst away,
And keep them from the sheep.
But if they rush dreadful;
The angels most heedful,
Recieve each mild spirit,
New worlds to inherit.

And there the lions ruddy eyes,
Shall flow with tears of gold:
And pitying the tender cries,
And walking round the fold:
Saying: wrath by his meekness
And by his health, sickness,
Is driven away,
From our immortal day.

And now beside thee bleating lamb,
I can lie down and sleep;
Or think on him who bore thy name,
Grase after thee and weep.
For wash'd in lifes river,
My bright mane for ever
Shall shine like the gold.
As I guard o'er the fold.

NURSE'S SONG

When the voices of children are heard on the green
And laughing is heard on the hill,
My heart is at rest within my breast
And every thing else is still

Then come home my children, the sun is gone down
And the dews of night arise
Come come leave off play, and let us away
Till the morning appears in the skies

No no let us play, for it is yet day
And we cannot go to sleep
Besides in the sky, the little birds fly
And the hills are all covered with sheep

Well well go & play till the light fades away
And then go home to bed
The little ones leaped & shouted & laugh'd
And all the hills ecchoed

INFANT JOY

I have no name
I am but two days old. –
What shall I call thee?
I happy am
Joy is my name, –
Sweet joy befall thee!

Pretty joy!
Sweet joy but two days old.
Sweet joy I call thee:
Thou dost smile.
I sing the while
Sweet joy befall thee.

A DREAM

Once a dream did weave a shade,
O'er my Angel-guarded bed,
That an Emmet lost its way
Where on grass methought I lay.

Troubled wildered and folorn
Dark benighted travel-worn,
Over many a tangled spray
All heart-broke I heard her say.

O my children! do they cry
Do they hear their father sigh.
Now they look abroad to see,
Now return and weep for me.

Pitying I drop'd a tear:
But I saw a glow-worm near:
Who replied: What wailing wight
Calls the watchman of the night.

I am set to light the ground,
While the beetle goes his round:
Follow now the beetles hum,
Little wanderer hie thee home.

ON ANOTHERS SORROW

Can I see anothers woe,
And not be in sorrow too.
Can I see anothers grief,
And not seek for kind relief.

Can I see a falling tear,
And not feel my sorrows share,
Can a father see his child,
Weep, nor be with sorrow fill'd.

Can a mother sit and hear,
An infant groan an infant fear –
No no never can it be.
Never never can it be.

And can he who smiles on all
Hear the wren with sorrows small,
Hear the small birds grief & care
Hear the woes that infants bear –

And not sit beside the nest
Pouring pity in their breast,
And not sit the cradle near
Weeping tear on infants tear.

And not sit both night & day,
Wiping all our tears away.
O! no never can it be.
Never never can it be.

He doth give his joy to all.
He becomes an infant small.
He becomes a man of woe
He doth feel the sorrow too.

Think not, thou canst sigh a sigh,
And thy maker is not by.
Think not, thou canst weep a tear,
And thy maker is not near.

O! he gives to us his joy,
That our grief he may destroy
Till our grief is fled & gone
He doth sit by us and moan

SONGS OF EXPERIENCE

INTRODUCTION

Hear the voice of the Bard!
Who Present, Past, & Future sees
Whose ears have heard,
The Holy Word,
That walk'd among the ancient trees.

Calling the lapsed Soul
And weeping in the evening dew:
That might controll,
The starry pole;
And fallen fallen light renew!

O Earth O Earth return!
Arise from out the dewy grass;
Night is worn,
And the morn
Rises from the slumberous mass.

Turn away no more:
Why wilt thou turn away
The starry floor
The watry shore
Is giv'n thee till the break of day.

EARTH'S ANSWER

Earth rais'd up her head,
From the darkness dread & drear.
Her light fled:
Stony dread!
And her locks cover'd with grey despair.

Prison'd on watry shore
Starry Jealousy does keep my den
Cold and hoar
Weeping o'er
I hear the Father of the ancient men

Selfish father of men
Cruel jealous selfish fear
Can delight
Chain'd in night
The virgins of youth and morning bear.

Does spring hide its joy
When buds and blossoms grow?
Does the sower
Sow by night?
Or the plowman in darkness plow?

Break this heavy chain,
That does freeze my bones around
Selfish! vain,
Eternal bane!
That free Love with bondage bound.

THE CLOD & THE PEBBLE

Love seeketh not Itself to please,
Nor for itself hath any care;
But for another gives its ease,
And builds a Heaven in Hells despair.

So sang a little Clod of Clay,
Trodden with the cattles feet:
But a Pebble of the brook,
Warbled out these metres meet:

Love seeketh only Self to please,
To bind another to its delight;
Joys in anothers loss of ease,
And builds a Hell in Heavens despite.

HOLY THURSDAY

Is this a holy thing to see,
In a rich and fruitful land,
Babes reduced to misery,
Fed with cold and usurous hand?

Is that trembling cry a song?
Can it be a song of joy?
And so many children poor?
It is a land of poverty!

And their sun does never shine.
And their fields are bleak & bare.
And their ways are fill'd with thorns.
It is eternal winter there.

For where-e'er the sun does shine,
And where-e'er the rain does fall:
Babe can never hunger there,
Nor poverty the mind appall.

THE LITTLE GIRL LOST

In futurity
I prophetic see,
That the earth from sleep,
(Grave the sentence deep)

Shall arise and seek
For her maker meek:
And the desart wild
Become a garden mild.

In the southern clime,
Where the summers prime,
Never fades away;
Lovely Lyca lay.

Seven summers old
Lovely Lyca told.
She had wanderd long,
Hearing wild birds song.

Sweet sleep come to me
Underneath this tree;
Do father, mother weep. –
'Where can Lyca sleep'.

Lost in desart wild
Is your little child.
How can Lyca sleep,
If her mother weep.

If her heart does ake,
Then let Lyca wake;
If my mother sleep,
Lyca shall not weep.

Frowning frowning night,
O'er this desart bright,
Let thy moon arise,
While I close my eyes.

Sleeping Lyca lay;
While the beasts of prey,
Come from caverns deep,
View'd the maid asleep

The kingly lion stood
And the virgin view'd,
Then he gambold round
O'er the hallowd ground:

Leopards, tygers play,
Round her as she lay;
While the lion old,
Bow'd his mane of gold.

And her bosom lick,
And upon her neck,
From his eyes of flame,
Ruby tears there came;

While the lioness,
Loos'd her slender dress,
And naked they convey'd
To caves the sleeping maid.

THE LITTLE GIRL FOUND

All the night in woe
Lyca's parents go:
Over vallies deep,
While the desarts weep.

Tired and woe-begone,
Hoarse with making moan:
Arm in arm seven days,
They trac'd the desart ways.

Seven nights they sleep,
Among shadows deep:
And dream they see their child
Starv'd in desart wild.

Pale thro pathless ways
The fancied image strays,
Famish'd, weeping, weak
With hollow piteous shriek

Rising from unrest,
The trembling woman prest,
With feet of weary woe;
She could no further go.

In his arms he bore,
Her arm'd with sorrow sore;
Till before their way,
A couching lion lay.

Turning back was vain,
Soon his heavy mane,
Bore them to the ground;
Then he stalk'd around,

Smelling to his prey.
But their fears allay,
When he licks their hands;
And silent by them stands.

They look upon his eyes
Fill'd with deep surprise:
And wondering behold,
A spirit arm'd in gold.

On his head a crown
On his shoulders down,
Flow'd his golden hair.
Gone was all their care.

Follow me he said,
Weep not for the maid;
In my palace deep,
Lyca lies asleep.

Then they followed,
Where the vision led:
And saw their sleeping child,
Among tygers wild.

To this day they dwell
In a lonely dell
Nor fear the wolvish howl,
Nor the lions growl.

THE CHIMNEY SWEEPER

A little black thing among the snow:
Crying weep, weep, in notes of woe!
Where are thy father & mother? say?
They are both gone up to the church to pray.

Because I was happy upon the heath
And smil'd among the winters snow:
They clothed me in the clothes of death.
And taught me to sing the notes of woe.

And because I am happy & dance & sing.
They think they have done me no injury:
And are gone to praise God & his Priest & King
Who make up a heaven of our misery.

NURSES SONG

When the voices of children are heard on the green
And whisperings are in the dale:
The days of my youth rise fresh in my mind,
My face turns green and pale.

Then come home my children, the sun is gone down
And the dews of night arise
Your spring & your day, are wasted in play
And your winter and night in disguise.

THE SICK ROSE

O Rose thou art sick.
The invisible worm,
That flies in the night
In the howling storm:

Has found out thy bed
Of crimson joy:
And his dark secret love
Does thy life destroy.

THE FLY

Little Fly
Thy summers play,
My thoughtless hand
Has brush'd away.

Am not I
A fly like thee?
Or art not thou
A man like me?

For I dance
And drink & sing;
Till some blind hand
Shall brush my wing.

If thought is life
And strength & breath;
And the want
Of thought is death;

Then am I
A happy fly,
If I live,
Or if I die.

THE TYGER

Tyger Tyger, burning bright,
In the forests of the night:
What immortal hand or eye,
Could frame thy fearful symmetry?

In what distant deeps or skies
Burnt the fire of thine eyes!
On what wings dare he aspire?
What the hand, dare sieze the fire?

And what shoulder, & what art,
Could twist the sinews of thy heart?
And when thy heart began to beat,
What dread hand? & what dread feet?

What the hammer? what the chain,
In what furnace was thy brain?
What the anvil? what dread grasp,
Dare its deadly terrors clasp?

When the stars threw down their spears
And water'd heaven with their tears:
Did he smile his work to see?
Did he who made the Lamb make thee?

Tyger, Tyger burning bright,
In the forests of the night:
What immortal hand or eye,
Dare frame thy fearful symmetry?

MY PRETTY ROSE TREE

A flower was offerd to me;
Such a flower as May never bore.
But I said I've a Pretty Rose-tree.
And I passed the sweet flower o'er.

Then I went to my Pretty Rose-tree;
To tend her by day and by night.
But my Rose turned away with jealousy:
And her thorns were my only delight.

AH! SUN-FLOWER

Ah Sun-flower! weary of time.
Who countest the steps of the Sun:
Seeking after that sweet golden clime
Where the travellers journey is done.

Where the Youth pined away with desire,
And the pale Virgin shrouded in snow:
Arise from their graves and aspire,
Where my Sun-flower wishes to go.

THE LILLY

The modest Rose puts forth a thorn:
The humble Sheep, a threatning horn:
While the Lilly white, shall in Love delight,
Nor a thorn nor a threat stain her beauty bright

LONDON

I wander thro' each charter'd street,
Near where the charter'd Thames does flow.
And mark in every face I meet
Marks of weakness, marks of woe.

In every cry of every Man,
In every Infants cry of fear,
In every voice: in every ban,
The mind-forg'd manacles I hear

How the Chimney-sweepers cry
Every blackning Church appalls,
And the hapless Soldiers sigh,
Runs in blood down Palace walls

But most thro' midnight streets I hear
How the youthful Harlots curse
Blasts the new-born Infants tear
And blights with plagues the Marriage hearse

THE HUMAN ABSTRACT

Pity would be no more,
If we did not make somebody Poor:
And Mercy no more could be,
If all were as happy as we;

And mutual fear brings peace;
Till the selfish loves increase.
Then Cruelty knits a snare,
And spreads his baits with care.

He sits down with holy fears,
And waters the ground with tears:
Then Humility takes its root
Underneath his foot.

Soon spreads the dismal shade
Of Mystery over his head;
And the Catterpilier and Fly,
Feed on the Mystery.

And it bears the fruit of Deceit,
Ruddy and sweet to eat;
And the Raven his nest has made
In its thickest shade.

The Gods of the earth and sea,
Sought thro' Nature to find this Tree
But their search was all in vain:
There grows one in the Human Brain

INFANT SORROW

My mother groand! my father wept.
Into the dangerous world I leapt:
Helpless, naked, piping loud;
Like a fiend hid in a cloud.

Struggling in my fathers hands:
Striving against my swadling bands:
Bound and weary I thought best
To sulk upon my mothers breast.

A LITTLE BOY LOST

Nought loves another as itself
Nor venerates another so.
Nor is it possible to Thought
A greater than itself to know:

And Father, how can I love you,
Or any of my brothers more?
I love you like the little bird
That picks up crumbs around the door.

The Priest sat by and heard the child.
In trembling zeal he siez'd his hair:
He led him by his little coat:
And all admir'd the Priestly care.

And standing on the altar high,
Lo what a fiend is here! said he:
One who sets reason up for judge
Of our most holy Mystery.

The weeping child could not be heard.
The weeping parents wept in vain:
They strip'd him to his little shirt.
And bound him in an iron chain.

And burn'd him in a holy place,
Where many had been burn'd before:
The weeping parents wept in vain.
Are such things done on Albions shore.

A LITTLE GIRL LOST

Children of the future Age,
Reading this indignant page:
Know that in a former time,
Love! sweet Love! was thought a crime.

In the Age of Gold,
Free from winters cold:
Youth and maiden bright,
To the holy light,
Naked in the sunny beams delight.

Once a youthful pair
Fill'd with softest care:
Met in garden bright,
Where the holy light,
Had just remov'd the curtains of the night.

There in rising day,
On the grass they play:
Parents were afar:
Strangers came not near:
And the maiden soon forgot her fear.

Tired with kisses sweet
They agree to meet,
When the silent sleep
Waves o'er heavens deep;
And the weary tired wanderers weep.

To her father white
Came the maiden bright:
But his loving look.
Like the holy book,
All her tender limbs with terror shook.

Ona! pale and weak!
To thy father speak:
O the trembling fear!
O the dismal care!
That shakes the blossoms of my hoary hair

TO TIRZAH

Whate'er is Born of Mortal Birth,
Must be consumed with the Earth
To rise from Generation free;
Then what have I to do with thee?

The Sexes sprung from Shame & Pride
Blow'd in the morn: in evening died
But Mercy changd Death into Sleep;
The Sexes rose to work & weep.

Thou Mother of my Mortal part
With cruelty didst mould my Heart,
And with false self-deceiving tears,
Didst bind my Nostrils Eyes & Ears.

Didst close my Tongue in senseless clay
And me to Mortal Life betray:
The Death of Jesus set me free,
Then what have I to do with thee?

THE VOICE OF THE ANCIENT BARD

Youth of delight come hither:
And see the opening morn,
Image of truth new born
Doubt is fled & clouds of reason
Dark disputes & artful teazing.
Folly is an endless maze,
Tangled roots perplex her ways,
How many have fallen there!
They stumble all night over bones of the dead;
And feel they know not what but care;
And wish to lead others when they should be led.

From THE NOTEBOOKS

Never pain to tell thy love
Love that never told can be
For the gentle wind does move
Silently invisibly

I told my love I told my love
I told her all my heart
Trembling, cold, in ghastly fears
Ah she doth depart

Soon as she was gone from me
A traveller came by
Silently invisibly
He took her with a sigh

O was no deny

*   *

If you trap the moment before its ripe
The tears of repentance you'll certainly wipe
But if once you let the ripe moment go
You can never wipe off the tears of woe

ETERNITY

He who binds to himself a joy
Does the winged life destroy:
But he who kisses the joy as it flies
Lives in eternity's sun rise.

AUGURIES OF INNOCENCE

To see a World in a Grain of Sand
And a Heaven in a Wild Flower
Hold Infinity in the palm of your hand
And Eternity in an hour
A Robin Red breast in a Cage
Puts all Heaven in a Rage
A dove house filld with doves & Pigeons
Shudders Hell thro all its regions
A dog starvd at his Masters Gate
Predicts the ruin of the State
A Horse misusd upon the Road
Calls to Heaven for Human blood
Each outcry of the hunted Hare
A fibre from the Brain does tear
A Skylark wounded in the wing
A Cherubim does cease to sing
The Game Cock clipd & armd for fight
Does the Rising Sun affright
Every Wolfs & Lions howl
Raises from Hell a Human Soul
The wild deer wandring here & there
Keeps the Human Soul from Care
The Lamb misusd breeds Public strife
And yet forgives the Butchers Knife
The Bat that flits at close of Eve
Has left the Brain that wont Believe
The Owl that calls upon the Night

Speaks the Unbelievers fright
He who shall hurt the little Wren
Shall never be belovd by Men
He who the Ox to wrath has movd
Shall never be by Woman lovd
The wanton Boy that kills the Fly
Shall feel the Spiders enmity
He who torments the Chafers sprite
Weaves a Bower in endless Night
The Catterpiller on the Leaf
Repeats to thee thy Mothers grief
Kill not the Moth nor Butterfly
For the Last Judgment draweth nigh
He who shall train the Horse to War
Shall never pass the Polar Bar
The Beggers Dog & Widows Cat
Feed them & thou wilt grow fat
The Gnat that sings his Summers song
Poison gets from Slanders tongue
The poison of the Snake & Newt
Is the sweat of Envys Foot
The Poison of the Honey Bee
Is the Artists Jealousy
The Princes Robes & Beggars Rags
Are Toadstools on the Misers Bags
A truth thats told with bad intent
Beats all the Lies you can invent
It is right it should be so
Man was made for Joy & Woe

And when this we rightly know
Thro the World we safely go
Joy & Woe are woven fine
A Clothing for the Soul divine
Under every grief & pine
Runs a joy with silken twine
The Babe is more than swadling Bands
Throughout all these Human Lands
Tools were made & Born were hands
Every Farmer Understands
Every Tear from Every Eye
Becomes a Babe in Eternity
This is caught by Females bright
And returnd to its own delight
The Bleat the Bark Bellow & Roar
Are Waves that Beat on Heavens Shore
The Babe that weeps the Rod beneath
Writes Revenge in realms of death
The Beggars Rags fluttering in Air
Does to Rags the Heavens tear
The Soldier armd with Sword & Gun
Palsied strikes the Summers Sun
The poor Mans Farthing is worth more
Than all the Gold on Africs Shore
One Mite wrung from the Labrers hands
Shall buy & sell the Misers Lands
Or if protected from on high
Does that whole Nation sell & buy
He who mocks the Infants Faith

Shall be mock'd in Age & Death
He who shall teach the Child to Doubt
The rotting Grave shall neer get out
He who respects the Infants faith
Triumphs over Hell & Death
The Childs Toys & the Old Mans Reasons
Are the Fruits of the Two seasons
The Questioner who sits so sly
Shall never know how to Reply
He who replies to words of Doubt
Doth put the Light of Knowledge out
The Strongest Poison ever known
Came from Caesars Laurel Crown
Nought can deform the Human Race
Like to the Armours iron brace
When Gold & Gems adorn the Plow
To peaceful Arts shall Envy Bow
A Riddle or the Crickets Cry
Is to Doubt a fit Reply
The Emmets Inch & Eagles Mile
Make Lame Philosophy to smile
He who Doubts from what he sees
Will neer Believe do what you Please
If the Sun & Moon should doubt
Theyd immediately Go out
To be in a Passion you Good may do
But no Good if a Passion is in you
The Whore & Gambler by the State
Licencd build that Nations Fate

The Harlots cry from Street to Street
Shall weave Old Englands winding Sheet
The Winners Shout the Losers Curse
Dance before dead Englands Hearse
Every Night & every Morn
Some to Misery are Born
Every Morn & every Night
Some are Born to sweet delight
Some are Born to sweet delight
Some are Born to Endless Night
We are led to Believe a Lie
When we see not Thro the Eye
Which was Born in a Night to perish in a Night
When the Soul Slept in Beams of Light
God Appears & God is Light
To those poor Souls who dwell in Night
But does a Human Form Display
To those who Dwell in Realms of day

THE MENTAL TRAVELLER

I traveld thro' a Land of Men
A Land of Men & Women too
And heard & saw such dreadful things
As cold Earth wanderers never knew

For there the Babe is born in joy
That was begotten in dire woe
Just as we Reap in joy the fruit
Which we in bitter tears did sow

And if the Babe is born a Boy
He's given to a Woman Old
Who nails him down upon a rock
Catches his shrieks in cups of gold

She binds iron thorns around his head
She pierces both his hands & feet
She cuts his heart out at his side
To make it feel both cold & heat

Her fingers number every Nerve
Just as a Miser counts his gold
She lives upon his shrieks & cries
And she grows young as he grows old

Till he becomes a bleeding youth
And she becomes a Virgin bright
Then he rends up his Manacles
And binds her down for his delight

He plants himself in all her Nerves
Just as a Husbandman his mould
And she becomes his dwelling place
And Garden fruitful seventy fold

An aged Shadow soon he fades
Wandring round an Earthly Cot
Full filled all with gems & gold
Which he by industry had got

And these are the gems of the Human Soul
The rubies & pearls of a lovesick eye
The countless gold of the akeing heart
The martyrs groan & the lovers sigh

They are his meat they are his drink
He feeds the Beggar & the Poor
And the wayfaring Traveller
For ever open is his door

His grief is their eternal joy
They make the roofs & walls to ring
Till from the fire on the hearth
A little Female Babe does spring

And she is all of solid fire
And gems & gold that none his hand
Dares stretch to touch her Baby form
Or wrap her in his swaddling-band

But She comes to the Man she loves
If young or old or rich or poor
They soon drive out the aged Host
A Beggar at anothers door

He wanders weeping far away
Untill some other take him in
Oft blind & age-bent sore distrest
Untill he can a Maiden win

And to allay his freezing Age
The Poor Man takes her in his arms
The Cottage fades before his sight
The Garden & its lovely Charms

The Guests are scattered thro' the land
For the Eye altering alters all
The Senses roll themselves in fear
And the flat Earth becomes a Ball

The Stars Sun Moon all shrink away
A desart vast without a bound
And nothing left to eat or drink
And a dark desart all around

The honey of her Infant lips
The bread & wine of her sweet smile
The wild game of her roving Eye
Does him to Infancy beguile

For as he eats & drinks he grows
Younger & younger every day
And on the desart wild they both
Wander in terror & dismay

Like the wild Stag she flees away
Her fear plants many a thicket wild
While he pursues her night & day
By various arts of Love beguild

By various arts of Love & Hate
Till the wide desart planted oer
With Labyrinths of wayward Love
Where roams the Lion Wolf & Boar

Till he becomes a wayward Babe
And she a weeping Woman Old
Then many a Lover wanders here
The Sun & Stars are nearer rolld

The trees bring forth sweet Extacy
To all who in the desart roam
Till many a City there is Built
And many a pleasant Shepherds home

But when they find the frowning Babe
Terror strikes thro the region wide
They cry the Babe the Babe is Born
And flee away on Every side

For who dare touch the frowning form
His arm is witherd to its root
Lions Boars Wolves all howling flee
And every Tree does shed its fruit

And none can touch that frowning form
Except it be a Woman Old
She nails him down upon the Rock
And all is done as I have told

From VALA, OR THE FOUR ZOAS

1. *Enion and Tharmas*

Why wilt thou Examine every little fibre of my soul
Spreading them out before the Sun like Stalks of flax
    to dry
The infant joy is beautiful but its anatomy
Horrible Ghast & Deadly nought shalt thou find in it
But Death Despair & Everlasting brooding Melancholy

Thou wilt go mad with horror if thou dost Examine
    thus
Every moment of my secret hours Yea I know
That I have sinnd & that my Emanations are become
    harlots
I am already distracted at their deeds & if I look
Upon them more Despair will bring self murder on my
    soul
O Enion thou art thyself a root growing in hell
Tho thus heavenly beautiful to draw me to destruction

Sometimes I think thou art a flower expanding
Sometimes I think thou art fruit breaking from its bud
In dreadful dolor & pain & I am like an atom
A Nothing left in darkness yet I am an identity
I wish & feel & weep & groan Ah terrible terrible

2. Enion's Lament

Why does the Raven cry aloud and no eye pities her?
Why fall the Sparrow & the Robin in the foodless
  winter?
Faint! shivering they sit on leafless bush, or frozen
  stone

Wearied with seeking food across the snowy waste; the
  little
Heart, cold; and the little tongue consum'd, that once
  in thoughtless joy
Gave songs of gratitude to the waving corn fields
  round their nest.

Why howl the Lion & the Wolf? why do they roam
  abroad?
Deluded by the summers heat they sport in enormous
  love
And cast their young out to the hungry wilds &
  sandy desarts

Why is the Sheep given to the knife? the Lamb plays
  in the Sun
He starts! he hears the foot of Man! he says, Take
  thou my wool
But spare my life, but he knows not that the winter
  cometh fast.

The Spider sits in his labourd Web, eager watching for
  the Fly
Presently comes a famishd Bird & takes away the
  Spider
His Web is left all desolate, that his little anxious heart
So careful wove; & spread it out with sighs and
  weariness.

3. Terrific Urizen

Terrific Urizen strode above, in fear & pale dismay
He saw the indefinite space beneath & his soul shrunk
   with horror
His feet upon the verge of Non Existence; his voice
   went forth

Luvah & Vala trembling & shrinking, beheld the
   great Work master
And heard his Word! Divide ye bands influence by
   influence
Build we a Bower for heavens darling in the grizly
   deep
Build we the Mundane Shell around the Rock of
   Albion

The Bands of Heaven flew thro the air singing &
   shouting to Urizen
Some fix'd the anvil, some the loom erected, some the
   plow
And harrow formd & framd the harness of silver &
   ivory

The golden compasses, the quadrant & the rule &
   balance
They erected the furnaces, they formd the anvils of
   gold beaten in mills
Where winter beats incessant, fixing them firm on
   their base
The bellows began to blow & the Lions of Urizen
   stood round the anvil

And the leopards coverd with skins of beasts tended
   the roaring fires
Sublime distinct their lineaments divine of human
   beauty
The tygers of wrath called the horses of instruction
   from their mangers
They unloos'd them & put on the harness of gold &
   silver & ivory
In human forms distinct they stood round Urizen
   prince of Light
Petrifying all the Human Imagination into rock &
   sand
Groans ran along Tyburns brook and along the River
   of Oxford

Among the Druid Temples. Albion groand on
   Tyburns brook
Albion gave his loud death groan The Atlantic
   Mountains trembled
Aloft the Moon fled with a cry the Sun with streams
   of blood
From Albions Loins fled all Peoples and Nations of the
   Earth
Fled with the noise of Slaughter & the stars of heaven
   Fled
Jerusalem came down in a dire ruin over all the Earth
She fell cold from Lambeths Vales in groans & Dewy
The dew of anxious souls the death-sweat of the dying
In every pillard hall & arched roof of Albions skies
The brother & the brother bathe in blood upon the
   Severn
The Maiden weeping by. The father & the mother
   with
The Maidens father & her mother fainting over the
   body
And the Young Man the Murderer fleeing over the
   mountains

4. *Vala's Lament*

O Lord wilt thou not look upon our sore afflictions

Among these flames incessant labouring, our hard
masters laugh

At all our sorrow. We are made to turn the wheel for
water

To carry the heavy basket on our scorched shoulders,
to sift

The sand & ashes, & to mix the clay with tears &
repentance

I see not Luvah as of old I only see his feet

Like pillars of fire travelling thro darkness & non
entity

The times are now returned upon us, we have given
ourselves

To scorn and now are scorned by the slaves of our
enemies

Our beauty is coverd over with clay & ashes, & our
backs

Furrowd with whips, & our flesh bruised with the
heavy basket

Forgive us O thou piteous one whom we have
offended, forgive

The weak remaining shadow of Vala that returns in
sorrow to thee.

5. Enion's Second Lament

I am made to sow the thistle for wheat; the nettle for a
  nourishing dainty
I have planted a false oath in the earth, it has brought
  forth a poison tree
I have chosen the serpent for a councellor & the dog
For a schoolmaster to my children
I have blotted out from light & living the dove &
  nightingale
And I have caused the earth worm to beg from door
  to door
I have taught the thief a secret path into the house of
  the just
I have taught pale artifice to spread his nets upon the
  morning
My heavens are brass my earth is iron my moon a
  clod of clay
My sun a pestilence burning at noon & a vapour of
  death in night

What is the price of Experience do men buy it for a
  song
Or wisdom for a dance in the street? No it is bought
  with the price
Of all that a man hath his house his wife his children
Wisdom is sold in the desolate market where none
  come to buy

And in the witherd field where the farmer plows for
   bread in vain

It is an easy thing to triumph in the summers sun
And in the vintage & to sing on the waggon loaded
   with corn
It is an easy thing to talk of patience to the afflicted
To speak the laws of prudence to the houseless
   wanderer

To listen to the hungry ravens cry in wintry season
When the red blood is filld with wine & with the
   marrow of lambs

It is an easy thing to laugh at wrathful elements
To hear the dog howl at the wintry door, the ox in
   the slaughter house moan
To see a god on every wind & a blessing on every
   blast
To hear sounds of love in the thunder storm that
   destroys our enemies house
To rejoice in the blight that covers his field, & the
   sickness that cuts off his children
While our olive & vine sing & laugh round our door
   & our children bring fruits & flowers

Then the groan & the dolor are quite forgotten & the
 slave grinding at the mill
And the captive in chains & the poor in the prison,
 & the soldier in the field
When the shatterd bone hath laid him groaning
 among the happier dead

It is an easy thing to rejoice in the tents of prosperity
Thus could I sing & thus rejoice, but it is not so with
 me!

6. Enion, from the Caverns of the Grave

Fear not O poor forsaken one O land of briars &
thorns

Where once the Olive flourishd & the Cedar spread
his wings

Once I waild desolate like thee my fallow fields in fear

Cried to the Churchyards & the Earthworm came in
dismal state

I found him in my bosom & I said the time of Love

Appears upon the rocks & hills in silent shades but
soon

A voice came in the night a midnight cry upon the
mountains

Awake the bridegroom cometh I awoke to sleep no
more

But an Eternal Consummation is dark Enion

The watry Grave. O thou Corn field O thou
Vegetater happy

More happy is the dark consumer hope drowns all my
torment

For I am now surrounded by a shadowy vortex
drawing

The Spectre quite away from Enion that I die a death

Of better hope altho I consume in these raging waters

The furrowd field replies to the grave I hear her reply
to me

Behold the time approaches fast that thou shalt be as
    a thing
Forgotten when one speaks of thee he will not be
    believd
When the man gently fades away in his immortality
When the mortal disappears in improved knowledge
    cast away
The former things so shall the Mortal gently fade away
And so become invisible to those who still remain
Listen I will tell thee what is done in the caverns of
    the grave
The Lamb of God has rent the Veil of Mystery soon
    to return
In Clouds & Fires around the rock & the Mysterious
    tree
As the seed waits Eagerly watching for its flower &
    fruit
Anxious its little soul looks out into the clear expanse
To see if hungry winds are abroad with their invisible
    army
So Man looks out in tree & herb & fish & bird &
    beast
Collecting up the scattered portions of his immortal
    body
Into the Elemental forms of every thing that grows
He tries the sullen north wind riding on its angry
    furrows

The sultry south when the sun rises & the angry east

When the sun sets when the clods harden & the cattle
stand

Drooping & the birds hide in their silent nests, he
stores his thoughts

As in a store house in his memory he regulates the
forms

Of all beneath & all above & in the gentle West

Reposes where the Suns heat dwells he rises to the
Sun

And to the Planets of the Night & to the stars that
gild

The Zodiac & the stars that sullen stand to north &
south

He touches the remotest pole & in the Center weeps

That Man should Labour & sorrow & learn & forget
& return

To the dark valley whence he came to begin his
labours anew

In pain he sighs in pain he labours in his universe

Screaming in birds over the deep & howling in the
Wolf

Over the slain & moaning in the cattle & in the
winds

And weeping over Orc & Urizen in clouds & dismal
flaming fires

And in the cries of birth & in the groans of death his
voice

Is heard throughout the Universe whereever a grass
    grows
Or a leaf buds The Eternal Man is seen is heard is felt
And all his Sorrows till he reassumes his ancient bliss

7. Vala's Song

Rise up O Sun most glorious minister & light of day

Flow on ye gentle airs & bear the voice of my
rejoicing

Wave freshly clear waters flowing around the tender
grass

And thou sweet smelling ground put forth thy life in
fruits & flowers

Follow me O my flocks & hear me sing my rapturous
Song

I will cause my voice to be heard on the clouds that
glitter in the sun

I will call & who shall answer me I will sing who shall
reply

For from my pleasant hills behold the living living
springs

Running among my green pastures delighting among
my trees

I am not here alone my flocks you are my brethren

And you birds that sing & adorn the sky you are my
    sisters
I sing & you reply to my Song I rejoice & you are
    glad
Follow me O my flocks we will now descend into the
    valley
O how delicious are the grapes flourishing in the Sun
How clear the spring of the rock running among the
    golden sand
How cool the breezes of the vally & the arms of the
    branching trees
Cover us from the sun come & let us sit in the Shade
My Luvah here hath placd me in a Sweet & pleasant
    Land
And given me fruits & pleasant waters & warm hills
    & cool valleys
Here will I build myself a house & here Ill call on his
    name
Here Ill return when I am weary & take my pleasant
    rest

THE SMILE

There is a Smile of Love
And there is a Smile of Deceit
And there is a Smile of Smiles
In which these two Smiles meet

And there is a Frown of Hate
And there is a Frown of disdain
And there is a Frown of Frowns
Which you strive to forget in vain

For it sticks in the Hearts deep Core
And it sticks in the deep Back bone
And no Smile that ever was smild
But only one Smile alone

That betwixt the Cradle & Grave
It only once Smild can be
But when it once is Smild
Theres an end to all Misery

THE GOLDEN NET

Three Virgins at the break of day
Whither young Man whither away
Alas for woe! alas for woe!
They cry & tears for ever flow
The one was Clothd in flames of fire
The other Clothd in iron wire
The other Clothd in tears & sighs
Dazling bright before my Eyes
They bore a Net of Golden twine
To hang upon the Branches fine
Pitying I wept to see the woe
That Love & Beauty undergo
To be consumd in burning Fires
And in ungratified desires
And in tears clothd Night & day
Melted all my Soul away
When they saw my Tears a Smile
That did Heaven itself beguile
Bore the Golden Net aloft
As on downy Pinions soft
Over the Morning of my day
Underneath the Net I stray
Now intreating Burning Fire
Now intreating Iron Wire
Now intreating Tears & Sighs
O when will the morning rise

THE LAND OF DREAMS

Awake awake my little Boy
Thou wast thy Mothers only joy
Why dost thou weep in thy gentle sleep
Awake thy Father does thee keep

O what Land is the Land of Dreams
What are its Mountains & what are its Streams
O Father I saw my Mother there
Among the Lillies by waters fair

Among the Lambs clothed in white
She walkd with her Thomas in sweet delight
I wept for joy like a dove I mourn
O when shall I again return

Dear Child I also by pleasant Streams
Have wanderd all Night in the Land of Dreams
But tho calm & warm the waters wide
I could not get to the other side

Father O Father what do we here
In this Land of unbelief & fear
The Land of Dreams is better far
Above the light of the Morning Star

MARY

Sweet Mary the first time she ever was there
Came into the Ball room among the Fair
The young Men & Maidens around her throng
And these are the words upon every tongue

An Angel is here from the heavenly Climes
Or again does return the Golden times
Her eyes outshine every brilliant ray
She opens her lips tis the Month of May

Mary moves in soft beauty & conscious delight
To augment with sweet smiles all the joys of the Night
Nor once blushes to own to the rest of the Fair
That sweet Love & Beauty are worthy our care

In the Morning the Villagers rose with delight
And repeated with pleasure the joys of the night
And Mary arose among Friends to be free
But no Friend from henceforward thou Mary shalt see

Some said she was proud some calld her a whore
And some when she passed by shut to the door
A damp cold came oer her her blushes all fled
Her lillies & roses are blighted & shed

O why was I born with a different Face
Why was I not born like this Envious Race
Why did Heaven adorn me with bountiful hand
And then set me down in an envious Land

To be weak as a Lamb & smooth as a dove
And not to raise Envy is calld Christian Love
But if you raise Envy your Merits to blame
For planting such spite in the weak & the tame

I will humble my Beauty I will not dress fine
I will keep from the Ball & my Eyes shall not shine
And if any Girls Lover forsakes her for me
I'll refuse him my hand & from Envy be free

She went out in Morning attird plain & neat
Proud Marys gone Mad said the Child in the Street
She went out in Morning in plain neat attire
And came home in Evening bespatterd with mire

She trembled & wept sitting on the Bed side
She forgot it was Night & she trembled & cried
She forgot it was Night she forgot it was Morn
Her soft Memory imprinted with Faces of Scorn

With Faces of Scorn & with Eyes of disdain
Like foul Fiends inhabiting Marys mild Brain
She remembers no Face like the Human Divine
All Faces have Envy sweet Mary but thine

And thine is a Face of sweet Love in Despair
And thine is a Face of mild sorrow & care
And thine is a Face of wild terror & fear
That shall never be quiet till laid on its bier

THE CRYSTAL CABINET

The Maiden caught me in the Wild
Where I was dancing merrily
She put me into her Cabinet
And Lockd me up with a golden Key

This Cabinet is formd of Gold
And Pearl & Crystal shining bright
And within it opens into a World
And a little lovely Moony Night

Another England there I saw
Another London with its Tower
Another Thames & other Hills
And another pleasant Surrey Bower

Another Maiden like herself
Translucent lovely shining clear
Threefold each in the other closd
O what a pleasant trembling fear

O what a smile a threefold Smile
Filld me that like a flame I burnd
I bent to Kiss the lovely Maid
And found a Threefold Kiss returnd

I strove to sieze the inmost Form
With ardor fierce & hands of flame
But burst the Crystal Cabinet
And like a Weeping Babe became

A weeping Babe upon the wild
And Weeping Woman pale reclind
And in the outward air again
I filld with woes the passing Wind

WILLIAM BOND

I wonder whether the Girls are mad
And I wonder whether they mean to kill
And I wonder if William Bond will die
For assuredly he is very ill

He went to Church in a May morning
Attended by Fairies one two & three
But the Angels of Providence drove them away
And he returnd home in Misery

He went not out to the Field nor Fold
He went not out to the Village nor Town
But he came home in a black black cloud
And took to his Bed & there lay down

And an Angel of Providence at his Feet
And an Angel of Providence at his Head
And in the midst a Black Black Cloud
And in the midst the Sick Man on his Bed

And on his Right hand was Mary Green
And on his Left hand was his Sister Jane
And their tears fell thro the black black Cloud
To drive away the sick mans pain

O William if thou dost another Love
Dost another Love better than poor Mary
Go & take that other to be thy Wife
And Mary Green shall her Servant be

Yes Mary I do another Love
Another I Love far better than thee
And Another I will have for my Wife
Then what have I to do with thee

For thou art Melancholy Pale
And on thy Head is the cold Moons shine
But she is ruddy & bright as day
And the sun beams dazzle from her eyne

Mary trembled & Mary chilld
And Mary fell down on the right hand floor
That William Bond & his Sister Jane
Scarce could recover Mary more

When Mary woke & found her Laid
On the Right hand of her William dear
On the Right hand of his loved Bed
And saw her William Bond so near

The Fairies that fled from William Bond
Danced around her Shining Head
They danced over the Pillow white
And the Angels of Providence left the Bed

I thought Love livd in the hot sun shine
But O he lives in the Moony light
I thought to find Love in the heat of day
But sweet Love is the Comforter of Night

Seek Love in the Pity of others Woe
In the gentle relief of anothers care
In the darkness of night & the winters snow
In the naked & outcast Seek Love there

From VISIONS OF THE DAUGHTERS OF ALBION

But when the morn arose, her lamentation renewd,
The Daughters of Albion hear her woes, & eccho
   back her sighs.

O Urizen! Creator of men! mistaken Demon of
   heaven:
Thy joys are tears! thy labour vain, to form men to
   thine image.
How can one joy absorb another? are not different
   joys
Holy, eternal, infinite! and each joy is a Love.

Does not the great mouth laugh at a gift? & the
   narrow eyelids mock
At the labour that is above payment, and wilt thou
   take the ape
For thy councellor? or the dog, for a schoolmaster to
   thy children?
Does he who contemns poverty, and he who turns
   with abhorrence
From usury: feel the same passion or are they moved
   alike?
How can the giver of gifts experience the delights of
   the merchant?
How the industrious citizen the pains of the
   husbandman

How different far the fat fed hireling with hollow
  drum;
Who buys whole corn fields into wastes, and sings
  upon the heath:
How different their eye and ear! how different the
  world to them!
With what sense does the parson claim the labour of
  the farmer?
What are his nets & gins & traps & how does he
  surround him
With cold floods of abstraction, and with forests of
  solitude,
To build him castles and high spires where kings &
  priests may dwell.
Till she who burns with youth and knows no fixed lot;
  is bound
In spells of law to one she loaths: and must she drag
  the chain
Of life, in weary lust: must chilling murderous
  thoughts, obscure
The clear heaven of her eternal spring? to bear the
  wintry rage
Of a harsh terror driv'n to madness, bound to hold a
  rod
Over her shrinking shoulders all the day; & all the
  night
To turn the wheel of false desire: and longings that
  wake her womb

To the abhorred birth of cherubs in the human form
That live a pestilence & die a meteor & are no more.
Till the child dwell with one he hates, and do the
  deed he loaths
And the impure scourge force his seed into its unripe
  birth
E'er yet his eyelids can behold the arrows of the day.

Does the whale worship at thy footsteps as the hungry
  dog?
Or does he scent the mountain prey, because his
  nostrils wide
Draw in the ocean? does his eye discern the flying cloud
As the ravens eye? or does he measure the expanse
  like the vulture?
Does the still spider view the cliffs where eagles hide
  their young?
Or does the fly rejoice, because the harvest is brought
  in?
Does not the eagle scorn the earth & despise the
  treasures beneath?
But the mole knoweth what is there, & the worm
  shall tell it thee.
Does not the worm erect a pillar in the mouldering
  church yard?
And a palace of eternity in the jaws of the hungry
  grave

Over his porch these words are written. Take thy bliss
   O Man!
And sweet shall be thy taste & sweet thy infant joys
   renew!

The morning comes, the night decays, the watchmen
 leave their stations;
The grave is burst, the spices shed, the linen wrapped
 up;
The bones of death, the cov'ring clay, the sinews
 shrunk & dry'd.
Reviving shake, inspiring move, breathing! awakening!
Spring like redeemed captives when their bonds &
 bars are burst;
Let the slave grinding at the mill, run out into the field:
Let him look up into the heavens & laugh in the
 bright air;
Let the inchained soul shut up in darkness and in
 sighing,
Whose face has never seen a smile in thirty weary
 years;
Rise and look out, his chains are loose, his dungeon
 doors are open.
And let his wife and children return from the
 opressors scourge;
They look behind at every step & believe it is a dream.
Singing. The Sun has left his blackness, & has found
 a fresher morning
And the fair Moon rejoices in the clear & cloudless
 night;
For Empire is no more, and now the Lion & Wolf
 shall cease.

From MILTON

1. 'Jerusalem'

And did those feet in ancient time
Walk upon Englands mountains green:
And was the holy Lamb of God,
On Englands pleasant pastures seen!

And did the Countenance Divine,
Shine forth upon our clouded hills?
And was Jerusalem builded here,
Among these dark Satanic Mills?

Bring me my Bow of burning gold:
Bring me my Arrows of desire:
Bring me my Spear: O clouds unfold!
Bring me my Chariot of fire!

I will not cease from Mental Fight,
Nor shall my Sword sleep in my hand:
Till we have built Jerusalem,
In Englands green & pleasant Land.

Thou hearest the Nightingale begin the Song of
   Spring;
The Lark sitting upon his earthy bed: just as the morn
Appears; listens silent; then springing from the waving
   Corn-field! loud
He leads the Choir of the Day: trill, trill, trill, trill,
Mounting upon the wings of light into the Great
   Expanse:
Reecchoing against the lovely blue & shining heavenly
   Shell:
His little throat labours with inspiration; every feather
On throat & breast & wings vibrates with the
   effluence Divine
All Nature listens silent to him & the awful Sun
Stands still upon the Mountain looking on this little
   Bird
With eyes of soft humility, & wonder love & awe.
Then loud from their green covert all the Birds begin
   their Song
The Thrush, the Linnet & the Goldfinch, Robin &
   the Wren
Awake the Sun from his sweet reverie upon the
   Mountain:
The Nightingale again assays his song & thro the day,
And thro the night warbles luxuriant; every Bird of
   Song
Attending his loud harmony with admiration & love.

This is a Vision of the lamentation of Beulah over
  Ololon!

Thou percievest the Flowers put forth their precious
  Odours!
And none can tell how from so small a center comes
  such sweets
Forgetting that within that Center Eternity expands
Its ever during doors, that Og & Anak fiercely guard.
First eer the morning breaks joy opens in the flowery
  bosoms
Joy even to tears, which the Sun rising dries; first the
  Wild Thyme
And Meadow-sweet downy & soft waving among the
  reeds.
Light springing on the air lead the sweet Dance: they
  wake
The Honeysuckle sleeping on the Oak: the flaunting
  beauty
Revels along upon the wind; the White-thorn lovely
  May
Opens her many lovely eyes: listening the Rose still
  sleeps
None dare to wake her; soon she bursts her crimson
  curtaind bed
And comes forth in the majesty of beauty; every
  Flower:
The Pink, the Jessamine, the Wall-flower, the
  Carnation

The Jonquil, the mild Lilly opes her heavens: every
   Tree,
And Flower & Herb soon fill the air with an
   innumerable Dance
Yet all in order sweet & lovely, Men are sick with
   Love!

When I first Married you, I gave you all my whole
    Soul
I thought that you would love my loves & joy in my
    delights
Seeking for pleasures in my pleasures O Daughter of
    Babylon
Then thou wast lovely, mild & gentle. now thou art
    terrible
In jealousy & unlovely in my sight, because thou hast
    cruelly
Cut off my loves in fury till I have no love left for thee
Thy love depends on him thou lovest & on his dear
    loves
Depend thy pleasures which thou hast cut off by
    jealousy
Therefore I shew my Jealousy & set before you Death.

From JERUSALEM 1.

And many conversed on these things as they labourd
    at the furrow
Saying: It is better to prevent misery, than to release
    from misery
It is better to prevent error, than to forgive the
    criminal:
Labour well the Minute Particulars, attend to the
    Little-ones:
And those who are in misery cannot remain so long
If we do but our duty: labour well the teeming Earth.

They Plow'd in tears, the trumpets sounded before the
    golden Plow
And the voices of the Living Creatures were heard in
    the clouds of heaven
Crying: Compell the Reasoner to Demonstrate with
    unhewn Demonstrations
Let the Indefinite be explored, and let every Man be
    Judged
By his own Works. Let all Indefinites be thrown into
    Demonstrations
To be pounded to dust & melted in the Furnaces of
    Affliction:
He who would do good to another, must do it in
    Minute Particulars
General Good is the plea of the scoundrel hypocrite &
    flatterer:

For Art & Science cannot exist but in minutely
   organized Particulars
And not in generalizing Demonstrations of the
   Rational Power.
The Infinite alone resides in Definite & Determinate
   Identity
Establishment of Truth depends on destruction of
   Falshood continually
On Circumcision: not on Virginity, O Reasoners of
   Albion

So cried they at the Plow. Albions Rock frowned
   above
And the Great Voice of Eternity rolled above terrible
   in clouds
Saying Who will go forth for us! & Who shall we send
   before our face?

From JERUSALEM

2. *To the Jews*

The fields from Islington to Marybone,
To Primrose Hill and Saint Johns Wood:
   Were builded over with pillars of gold,
And there Jerusalems pillars stood.

   Her Little-ones ran on the fields
The Lamb of God among them seen
   And fair Jerusalem his Bride:
Among the little meadows green.

   Pancrass & Kentish-town repose
Among her golden pillars high:
   Among her golden arches which
Shine upon the starry sky.

   The Jews-harp-house & the Green Man;
The Ponds where Boys to bathe delight:
   The fields of Cows by Willans farm:
Shine in Jerusalems pleasant sight.

   She walks upon our meadows green:
The Lamb of God walks by her side:
   And every English Child is seen,
Children of Jesus & his Bride,

Forgiving trespasses and sins
Lest Babylon with cruel Og,
　　With Moral & Self-righteous Law
Should Crucify in Satans Synagogue!

　　What are those golden Builders doing
Near mournful ever-weeping Paddington
　　Standing above that mighty Ruin
Where Satan the first victory won.

　　Where Albion slept beneath the Fatal Tree
And the Druids golden Knife,
　　Rioted in human gore,
In Offerings of Human Life

　　They groan'd aloud on London Stone
They groan'd aloud on Tyburns Brook
　　Albion gave his deadly groan,
And all the Atlantic Mountains shook

　　Albions Spectre from his Loins
Tore forth in all the pomp of War!
　　Satan his name: in flames of fire
He stretch'd his Druid Pillars far.

Jerusalem fell from Lambeth's Vale,
Down thro Poplar & Old Bow;
Thro Malden & acros the Sea,
In War & howling death & woe.

The Rhine was red with human blood:
The Danube rolld a purple tide:
On the Euphrates Satan stood:
And over Asia stretch'd his pride.

He witherd up sweet Zions Hill,
From every Nation of the Earth:
He withered up Jerusalems Gates,
And in a dark Land gave her birth.

He witherd up the Human Form,
By laws of sacrifice for sin:
Till it became a Mortal Worm:
But O! translucent all within.

The Divine Vision still was seen
Still was the Human Form, Divine
    Weeping in weak & mortal clay
O Jesus still the Form was thine.

    And thine the Human Face & thine
The Human Hands & Feet & Breath
    Entering thro' the Gates of Birth
And passing thro' the Gates of Death

    And O thou Lamb of God, whom I
Slew in my dark self-righteous pride:
    Art thou return'd to Albions Land!
And is Jerusalem thy Bride?

    Come to my arms & never more
Depart; but dwell for ever here:
    Create my Spirit to thy Love:
Subdue my Spectre to thy Fear.

Spectre of Albion! warlike Fiend!
In clouds of blood & ruin roll'd:
    I here reclaim thee as my own
My Selfhood! Satan! armd in gold.

    Is this thy soft Family-Love
Thy cruel Patriarchal pride
    Planting thy Family alone,
Destroying all the World beside.

    A mans worst enemies are those
Of his own house & family;
    And he who makes his law a curse,
By his own law shall surely die.

    In my Exchanges every Land
Shall walk, & mine in every Land,
    Mutual shall build Jerusalem:
Both heart in heart & hand in hand.

EPIGRAPH TO THE CHRISTIANS

I give you the end of a golden string,
   Only wind it into a ball:
It will lead you in at
   Heavens gate,
Built in Jerusalems wall.

EPILOGUE

To the Accuser who Is the God of this World

Truly My Satan thou art but a Dunce
And dost not know the Garment from the Man
Every Harlot was a Virgin once
Nor canst thou ever change Kate into Nan

Tho thou art Worshipd by the Names Divine
Of Jesus & Jehovah: thou art still
The Son of Morn in weary Nights decline
The lost Travellers Dream under the Hill